Gideon — The Youngest Wagon Driver

A story based upon the true account
of a pioneer boy who crossed the plains in 1847

A Book for Children of all Ages—and their Grandparents

Dedicated to:

Those children of 1847 who crossed near half a continent,
brave and courageous, and wise beyond their tender years.
These little souls could not know the paths they followed led into
immortality—and deeply into our hearts.

This Book Belongs to:

A Gift from:

Date:

Gideon-The Youngest Wagon Driver

Other Gideon Stories...
Gideon's Baptism—A Day to Always Remember
Gideon and the Miracle of the Seagulls (coming soon)

Distributed by: Granite Publishing and Distribution
ISBN: 1-930980-71-X

Published by: Summerwood Publishers
2641 East 300 North
Layton, Utah 84040

Written by S. Reed Murdock
Illustrated by Sundri
Copyright © 2002 by S. Reed Murdock
All Rights Reserved
Printed in Korea

Council Bluffs, Iowa (1846)

You will like Gideon. He is a six-year-old boy living with his family in a small cabin in a place called Council Bluffs, Iowa on the banks of the Missouri River. The family recently came here from Nauvoo, Illinois with a large group of Mormon Pioneers, and they are waiting to go to the Rocky Mountains to make their permanent home.

A few months before the family left Nauvoo, Gideon's mother became very sick and died. Gideon misses her very much. Gideon also has two older brothers, Orrice and John R., but they have joined the Mormon Battalion to serve their country during difficulties with Mexico. So, Gideon is the oldest child at home and even though he is only six-years old, his father depends on him for many things.

There is much sickness and disease along the river and it brings death into nearly every home. Gideon's little brother, Hyrum, has recently died along with hundreds of others in the scattered settlements near Gideon's home.

Even though death and disease are everywhere, the pioneer settlements are filled with hope for the coming spring and the thought that they will be leaving soon for the valley beyond the great Rocky Mountains.

Gideon—The Youngest Wagon Driver

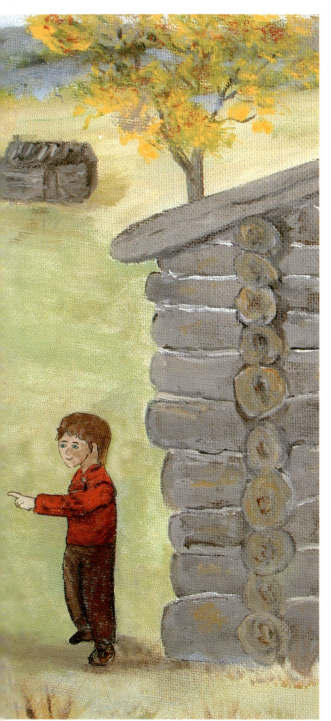

"Gideon," his father called from outside the cabin, "Can you come outside?" Gideon was just dressing; he finished pulling on his shoes and ran outside into the beautiful autumn morning. There he saw his father holding the ropes leading to two large oxen. "Remember Brother and Sister Cooper who died last week in the grove? The leaders have asked us to take their little daughter Mary into our family and they have asked us to take the Cooper wagon and team to the valley with extra supplies." Then Gideon's father looked at the two large animals and said, "This is Isaac and this is Samuel."

Gideon thought about the Coopers and felt bad that they had died. So many people were dying from the "river" disease. It made him think briefly about his own little brother, Hyrum, who was one of those who had died. Gideon's father continued, "We must have this team ready to make the journey in just a few weeks. We already have one wagon and you are now the oldest one in the family. I will need you to drive this extra team to the Rocky Mountains when the time comes. Do you think you can do that?"

Gideon could not believe what his father had just said. "Father, I'm only six-years old. Do you think I can do it?" His father looked at him thoughtfully. "Yes, Gideon, I believe you can. The team is older and quite gentle. Samuel here is a follower and will do most anything that Isaac does. Isaac is the leader and can be a little stubborn at times, but we will work with them. I will always be close by."

John continued, "There are no reins to stop the oxen or turn them. Many men lead the oxen with a rope by walking beside them, but because of your size, you will need to lead them with your voice command from the wagon. The oxen have learned when they hear the words 'Geehaw', they move forward. If you yell 'Gee', they turn to the right. 'Haw' makes them turn to the left and when you yell 'Whoa', they stop. Even though they know those commands, they must learn to hear and recognize the commands in your voice, before they will follow."

Gideon had heard the drivers yell "Gee" and "Haw" along the trail from Nauvoo to Council Bluffs. In fact, one day, when there was no one around, he had yelled the commands to a team of oxen and they just stood there and looked at him.

Gideon spent the next few days getting acquainted with the oxen. He soon shortened their names to "Izzy" and "Sam". Then one day he and his father, John, began working with the animals. At first, John would lead the oxen with a rope, and as Gideon would shout out "Gee", John would turn the oxen to the right. When Gideon yelled "Haw", John would turn the oxen to the left. When Gideon shouted "Whoa", John would stop the oxen. The oxen seemed to be getting the idea. Then, John would drive his own team and Gideon would follow with his team just behind. Izzy and Sam usually followed Gideon's commands as he shouted them from the driver's seat of the new wagon—but not always; Izzy would not always stop when he was supposed to.

The pioneers suffered through a cold and torturing winter, but spring had brought warm breezes and everything began to turn to green. May turned to June. It was time for the companies to head west. Brigham Young, the leader of the Mormons, had left the camp with a smaller group of pioneers a few weeks before. Now the larger group of wagons was ready to head west. The afternoon before their departure, hundreds of wagons assembled near a large clearing on the west side of the Missouri River near a place called Winter Quarters, Nebraska. Gideon was busy on the other side of the wagon when he noticed Captain Abraham Smoot, the leader of their 100 wagons, walking toward his father.

Captain Smoot reached out his hand to John, "Good morning, John. Who is going to drive your second wagon?" he asked.

Gideon stopped rolling his bedding and waited to hear his father's answer. "My son Gideon will drive the Cooper team," John answered.

"You can't mean that," Captain Smoot said. "I'm sure he is a fine boy, John, but he is just a child. As captain of this company, I am responsible for any problems or delays. Can't you find an older, more experienced driver for the team?"

After a moment, John spoke, "Abraham, I have sent two strong sons with the Mormon Battalion. There is no one else. I did not want to place such responsibility on Gideon, but I have no choice. He has been working hard with the team. He is doing a good job and I know he can do it."

Captain Smoot looked worried. "Well, if we have any problems, you may be asked to turn back and wait for a later group, so that you can locate an older and more experienced driver. I must think of the safety of the entire group."

John said, "I understand completely. We'll try not to let you down." As John turned toward the wagons, he caught Gideon looking his way and gave him a wink.

On the morning of June 7, 1847, the long line of wagons slowly climbed the gentle slopes leading west away from the Missouri River at Winter Quarters. Gideon's wagon followed closely behind the wagon driven by his father. Izzy and Sam seemed to know what they were to do and Gideon had no problems as his team joined the long procession of covered wagons. There was an excitement in the air and Gideon could feel it. They were heading for an unknown country and had no idea what adventure each new day would bring to them.

One morning shortly after the wagons had started moving for the day, Captain Smoot gave the order to stop so he could check on a problem with one of the first wagons in the line. The wagon train slowed and then stopped. But Izzy was not of a mind to stop just yet, and, of course, Sam followed right along.

Gideon yelled as loud as he could, "Whoa, Izzy! Whoa, Sam! Whoa! Whoa!" Still, the team would not stop. Gideon's wagon left the trail and turned to the left, barely missing a large rock, and then it bounced high in the air as the wheels passed over a small log at the side of the trail. Izzy, Sam, Gideon and the precious cargo of food, clothing and supplies headed over brush, rocks and anything that stood in their way.

Gideon knew what he must do. He had done it before when the team would not stop. He would jump from the wagon, run to the front of the oxen and grab Izzy's halter and hang on it until the oxen stopped. As Gideon jumped to the ground, his foot slipped and he fell in front of the wagon. The front wheel of the wagon passed over his legs. Gideon felt a sharp pain as the sharp edges of the wheel dug into his small limbs.

Brother Tom Call, one of the wagon drivers who was near by, ran to Izzy and Sam and stopped the team, while John rushed to his small son. "Gideon, are you alright? Can you move your legs?"

Gideon slowly stretched out on the dusty ground and wiggled his toes. "I believe I'm okay," he said, "The pain is not too bad and I can move them alright."

John held Gideon for a few moments. "You were blessed, Son. The soft soil helped to cushion your legs or they would have been broken by the wheel."

Gideon stood and turned toward the wagons just in time to see Captain Smoot on his large bay horse. He had a look of concern on his face. Captain Smoot said, "Is he well enough to continue?"

Gideon held back the tears as he silently nodded and headed back to his wagon. He thought, "I must be brave."

John answered, "I believe he will be fine; he was just shaken up a bit."

That afternoon, Gideon found his father working on a loose strap of the tailgate of his wagon. Gideon watched him as he worked and then said to his father, "I'm sorry about today, Father. Will Captain Smoot make us go back and wait for another company?"

"No, Son," his father answered. "We will just have to figure a way for the team to follow your commands, so that it doesn't happen again."

Gideon had been thinking. He spoke to his Father, "Some of the other drivers use whips. Do you think it would help if I did too?"

John smiled at Gideon. "Gideon, you have a special gift with animals. I first noticed it when you were very young and I have noticed it already on this journey. You have made friends with the rabbits along the trail. They seem to know that you will not harm them. The oxen are no different, just larger. Our Heavenly Father gives us these animals for a special purpose, and they understand much more than most people think. I know you will find a way to have Izzy and Sam follow you and you will never have to use a whip. You are doing a fine job and I am very proud of you. I know you will come up with a way to solve the problem. I will be there to help you and so will your Heavenly Father."

Gideon finished his meal and then walked over to the meadow where the oxen were being kept for the night. Izzy and Sam had their heads down and were enjoying some tender shoots of grass on the banks of a small meandering stream. Gideon had put some oats from the wagon in his pocket and offered a handful to Izzy as he patted him on the neck. "Izzy, you nearly got us sent home today. You are such a strong and smart animal. You've got to help us get to our new home." Gideon scratched the large animal behind his ears. Sam had nuzzled up close for his share of the oats and a little scratching as well. Gideon looked at the two large, gentle oxen and stroked the soft stubby hair on their noses.

A thought came to Gideon—he would ask his Heavenly Father for help. He walked to a private spot in the nearby meadow and knelt on the moist grass. "Heavenly Father, thank you for giving us a new home and thank you for Izzy and Sam. Please help me to be a good driver. I want to help us all get to our new home in safety. Please help Izzy understand how important it is for him to follow the rules and bless Sam to be a good follower. Please bless Captain Smoot that he won't make us go back."

Gideon finished his prayer and stood to his feet. As he turned, he saw both Izzy and Sam looking at him. Somehow, Gideon knew that things would turn out all right.

For the next few days, things seemed to go smoothly. Gideon remembered his prayer and wondered, "What can I do to be a better driver?" The thought came to Gideon, "I must be a friend to Izzy and Sam—a true friend."

Gideon spent every waking hour with the team; he made sure they always had plenty to eat; each night, after the company had stopped for the day and the animals had been unhooked from their wagons, he brushed them down and then walked with them to nearby meadows; he talked to them constantly so they would know his voice, patting their necks, as he did. The oxen started watching for Gideon and would walk toward him when he came into sight, expecting a treat or a scratch behind the ears.

Gideon missed being able to run off and play with the other boys his age at the end of the day, but he knew that it would not be long before he could join his friends; for now, his friends were Izzy and Sam.

The days that followed were warm and the trail was dry and smooth. The Smoot Company had not had any difficulty since Gideon's legs were run over, and, so far, Gideon's team had not caused any more problems. They usually followed his instructions as he shouted them from the wagon.

One day, soon after the company had started moving, a bright sun shone overhead. It was a beautiful day. Just then, a rider came by the wagon and warned that a large stream crossed the trail ahead. As Gideon's wagon approached the stream, he could hear the roar of the water. The teams could also hear the sound and they all seemed to sense the danger of the fast-moving stream ahead.

On this day, Gideon's wagon had been separated from that of his father's and he followed the wagon driven by the Widow Brown, whose husband had died at Winter Quarters, leaving her responsible for their two small daughters, Melissa, age nine and Mary, age five. Widow Brown had insisted on coming west and driving her own wagon.

At first, the waters at the edge of the stream were shallow and caused no problems for the wagons, but the streambed dropped off sharply and the swift waters began to rock and sway the wagons. Some of the animals balked at the power of the stream and had to be prodded to continue through the water.

The Widow Brown had managed to get her team most of the way across, when her oxen stepped into a large hole hidden under the rushing stream. Her team pressed forward into the hole two or three wagon-lengths, but finally panicked and stopped, while the fast-moving water caused the wagon to tip dangerously back and forth. Gideon recognized the problem. He could not let his team follow into the deep hole. He yelled to Izzy and Sam, "Gee, Izzy! Gee, Sam! Gee! Gee! Gee!" Izzy and Sam slowly turned to the right and pulled around the Widow Brown's stalled wagon—and the hole. The team continued to pull together up out of the strong current of the water onto dry ground. Gideon's heart was beating so hard that he could feel it in his ears.

Gideon stopped his team, reached into his wagon for a rope and jumped to the ground. He ran back into the water and waded into the edge of the stream and then climbed onto a large flat rock just under the water near the Widow Brown's team. He leaned out into the stream until he could barely reach the yoke of the Widow Brown's oxen. He managed to wrap a simple knot in the rope and hurried to the shore. He jerked and pulled until the oxen started to move slowly forward pulling the wagon from the deep water up onto the safe banks of the stream.

"Bless you, Gideon," the Widow Brown shouted as she directed her team to join the other wagons. Before Gideon climbed to his seat, he went to the head of his team and could be seen whispering into their ears and patting their dripping necks.

Gideon was exhausted as he sat around the campfire that afternoon. His father had heard about what had happened and the two of them had a good talk. Gideon knew that his father was very proud of him. Gideon gazed into the dancing flames of the dying fire.

Just then, a deep voice called from behind him, "Gideon, is that you?" Gideon jumped up to see the towering frame of Captain Smoot.

"Yes, Sir," Gideon replied.

Captain Smoot smiled and ruffled Gideon's hair, "I saw what you did today and I saw the way you handled your team. I just want you to know that you did a fine thing and I will not forget it." He gave Gideon a friendly slap on the back and said, "Get a good night's sleep, we have another big day tomorrow."

As Gideon finished his prayers and climbed into his bedroll, he locked his hands behind his head and gazed into the clear, starlit night. "Momma would have been proud of me today," he thought. A tear ran down his cheek as he drifted off into a deep restful sleep.

The days came rapidly. June and July passed quickly. It was now the first day of August and the company had made good progress. That night around the campfire, one of the men said, "Well, I understand this is a special day."

Gideon wondered what it was and then he was embarrassed as the entire group sang a birthday song to him. It was his seventh birthday and he had nearly forgotten. After the song, the two Brown girls, Melissa and Mary, made their way around the campfire. They had a small object wrapped in brown paper. Melissa smiled at Gideon and said, "This was our father's and we voted as a family that we wanted you to have it for your birthday."

Gideon fumbled with the paper and finally tore it loose to find the most beautiful pocketknife he had ever seen. It had an ivory handle and two blades, which were very sharp. It was a gift he would always treasure. He thanked Melissa and Mary and glanced toward the Widow Brown. He noticed her eyes were glistening as she smiled at him. The world seemed right and Heavenly Father was blessing the company.

For several days, the company made good progress across the prairie. They stayed close to a long gentle river, so water and grass were always abundant. Gradually, the ground began to slope upward to the West and they passed through small mountain ranges. Then, one clear, cloudless day, just as the company was getting a good start, Gideon heard a shout from the wagons ahead. Someone had spotted a long line of mountains on the horizon. Gideon looked and could see them clearly. They had come to the Rocky Mountains.

August had passed into September. Over the next few days, the wagons climbed into the mountains. Gideon had never seen anything so amazing. The high-mountain trees were changing colors. There were large boulders and deep canyons. It was a beautiful sight. The nights were turning cold; Gideon moved his bedroll to the shelter of the wagon and added an additional blanket.

Finally on a late September evening, Captain Smoot announced that this would be their last night on the trail and that they would enter the Valley of the Great Salt Lake early during the next day. Gideon was so excited he could hardly sleep during the night. The next morning after the usual prayers and breakfast, the teams were hooked to the wagons and the company started down the steep slopes leading to the valley.

As the company came to the opening in the mountains, Gideon could see a large lake in the distance and wondered where they would build their home. As they reached the valley floor, some of the pioneers who had arrived earlier were there to greet them. The wagons were led to a spot where the foothills leveled to a flat plain between the large lake and the towering mountains.

Captain Smoot called the company together in a final gathering. "Before we go our separate ways, I wanted to meet one last time and offer gratitude to the Lord for our safe arrival. I want to express to all of you my personal appreciation for having you in my company. Our paths may not cross again, but I will always remember each one of you with tender thoughts."

Captain Smoot then thanked all of the leaders in the company for their assistance to him and gave special mention to those who had made unusual sacrifices along the way. He then smiled and called Gideon to the front of the group.

Captain Smoot laid his large, rough hands on Gideon's small shoulders and said, "I guess most of you know that I had some serious concern about having such a young driver in my company, but I had no reason to worry. Gideon, I want to thank you for the example you set for all of us." Looking out at the company, Captain Smoot said, "I believe that Gideon will be known one day as the youngest pioneer to drive a team and wagon the entire distance from Winter Quarters to the Great Salt Lake Valley. I count it a great blessing in my life to have had this experience with such a fine young man."

Captain Smoot stuck out his hand and gave Gideon a handshake that the young boy would remember all of his life.

Gideon headed back through the crowd to his family when a gentle hand reached out and pulled him to one side. It was the Widow Brown. She gave Gideon a big hug and said, "And thank you from the Brown family for being an answer to a prayer we said in the middle of a rushing stream."

Gideon blushed, but felt a warmth in his heart for this special family. "I couldn't have done it without Izzy and Sam—and Heavenly Father."

John beamed as his son reached his side. Gideon looked up and asked, "What do we need to do now, Father?"

"You need to go off and play with your friends, Gideon. It is time for you to be a boy again," he smiled.

As Gideon left the wagons, he stopped by Izzy and Sam and whispered something in their ears—and then he was off to be with his other friends.

Notes

The story of Gideon is based on a true account of Gideon Allen Murdock contained in his journal, *Gideon Murdock, 1840-1925*, and the autobiography of his father, *John Murdock, An Abridged Record of the Life of John Murdock*, both maintained in the archives of the Church of Jesus Christ of Latter-day Saints, Historical Department, Salt Lake City, Utah.

Some of the detail of the story is fictional, however the following facts were revealed by the journals:

- Gideon's mother, Electa Allen Murdock, had died in Nauvoo, Illinois, a few months before the family left for Council Bluffs.
- Gideon drove a team and wagon the entire distance from Winter Quarters to the Salt Lake Valley and was likely the youngest teamster of the trek of 1847; he turned seven along the way.
- The extra wagon driven by Gideon had belonged to George and Alice Cooper, who died near Winter Quarters during the fall of 1846. The Cooper's daughter, Mary, was just eighteen months and was taken by the Murdocks and raised to adulthood, first by John and Sarah Murdock and later by John's son, John R. and his wife, Almira.
- Gideon's team and wagon and that of his father's were assigned to the company of 100 led by Abraham Smoot.
- There were instances during the trek when Gideon's feet and legs were run over by his wagon as he attempted to jump from the wagon to stop the oxen.
- Gideon grew to manhood, moved to Beaver, Utah where he married Lucinda Elvira Howd. They raised a large family and Gideon and Elvira served in positions of leadership in the Church and community. Gideon always had a special way with animals all of his life. He died at age 85 in Beaver, Utah in 1925 and was buried in the cemetery at Minersville, Utah where he and his family had lived for sometime.